9 LIFE
LESSONS

Finding Financial

Happiness on Your Terms

Carol Wysocki, Ph.D., CPA

ISBN-13: 978-1530478033

ISBN-10: 1530478030

Printed in the United States of America

Contents

Writing this book is a challenge as I continue to learn new things every year. I wrote this book because I could not find a Personal Finance book that dealt with emotions and other personal finance subjects that I consider important. We change over the decades as we age and hopefully we get wiser, more compassionate, and more thoughtful in our actions and words. I am sharing my story hoping that it will help you find your way to Financial peace and happiness quicker than me.

In my 20s my financial plan consisted of one goal of getting my MRS. or getting married. I wasn't studious and couldn't decide what I wanted to do in life. I finished a four-year degree in Food Technology due to my parent's insistence that I finish a degree to be able to support myself. My husband was the opposite of me and was very studious since he finished a PH.D degree in Agriculture so I planned on him supporting us with me helping out with part-time work. We had a family consisting of our son,

Byron, and our daughter, Amanda, while I was in my twenties so our family was complete. My financial plan of getting a man was my plan and it worked in that time era for me in my 20s.

In my 30s I tried various part-time jobs as we raised our family. Nothing seemed really interesting to me career wise as I worked in a soils lab and a flour lab testing stuff. We moved to a small town of Pendleton, Oregon with a steady population of 16,000 so few business opportunities were available. I knew that with a family I preferred not to work a lot of weekends and I wanted to work during the day so that narrowed down the possibilities. Finally-my husband told me to pick something and stick with it-just make a choice and stick with it. .

I did some tax work which was very seasonal but I wasn't super excited about that either. The business classes for a four-year degree came to town and so I started on those classes which were Friday nights from 5-9 pm. I realized I needed to find a business specialty that would work with a small town so I chose Accounting. It was a really good decision that I do over any day in a heartbeat. I enjoyed the work but decided to pursue an additional degree or my MBA or Master's degree in Business Administration which opened up new doors including teaching college classes. I was finally in a good place teaching accounting courses at the Community College. So at this point in my life I had not saved much money for my own pension but I had completed two degrees and had a good career. My husband had a pension and we had saved a little extra money in my 30s.

Onward to my 40s where I got the bright idea to get a Ph.D., like my husband, at my age-middle forties. Our children were in college and I wanted to return to college so it wasn't an optimal idea time to return to college. I completed a year and a half worth of classes which weren't very exciting to me. I wasn't convinced the benefits would be more than the cost so I returned to work and keep saving

for retirement. A few years later, I decided on a new path

to finish the Ph.D. degree because part of a degree is pretty

useless so I graduated in May before my 50th birthday in

October. So in my 40s I added another degree which

opened up new doors.

Finally, in my 50s I decided I really needed to get

serious about saving for my retirement. I had always saved

retirement money but I hadn't done in calculations and I

was just hoping there was enough in the account to retire

sometime. Well-there was money in the account but my

calculations showed it wouldn't go as far as I had hoped

and nothing would be left over for an inheritance? Now I

had the focus and the desire to really work on it and I

picked up extra gigs that went towards my savings goal. I

was relentless in my quest to get that money saved pre-tax

and reduce our taxes. Close to ten years later, I have been

making up for lost years of not saving enough mostly

because with raising a family there wasn't much money left to add to retirement. It's so much effort to stash or tuck away the money paycheck after paycheck but it gets easier over time. I discovered that you live on what you have so automatic savings payment is the way to go. Every year I put more money away and adjusted my standard of living to what I had to live on. Now with some dollar pinching, my retirement goal is within sight. It's pretty much like rolling a snowball-it takes forever to get it going and see returns don't seem like much until the numbers get bigger. Having reached my goal for retirement savings, I set new goals that I had never considered.

Dream big is one of my mantras-set your goals higher because you may reach them.

LESSON 1 EMOTIONS

The first of our lessons is about emotions and money since they influence our financial decisions. As a CPA I thought everyone made decisions based upon numbers without considering credit cards. The average credit card debt in this country is over $15,000 meaning that many people carry credit card balances. I have been very conservative in running our finances for over 35 years and we use credit cards knowing that we pay the balance off every month. I just can't pay those very high interest rates on top of the price of the item because I could save that money elsewhere.

It's now how much you make but how much you save that counts.

Most of us continue to learn throughout our lives and are a student of life. Life is a journey of lessons learned either the hard way or the easy way. Many life lessons are experiences that we learn from different situations especially in the area of money and personal finances. If I had only known or thought of that earlier in my life is what many of us say when we learn something new. I teach college level Personal Finance courses and older students wish they had the course or information so many years ago. Well we are learning it now so let's go forward together now.

We would like to think we can manage our finances simply by spending less than we make since it's rational and everyone can add and subtract. That sounds easy but then there are the wants and the emotions. We make many of our decisions rationally and emotionally although some decisions are totally based on emotions. Emotional wants or buying an item because it's the latest gadget isn't because we need it-it temporarily helps us feel good or comfortable.

Most of us have a perception that because someone lives in an expensive home or drives an elegant car they are wealthy. It's possible to be living next to a millionaire or someone going through bankruptcy and quite often we don't know what the situation is. Some people inherit a lot of money and choose to spend it conspicuously or invest it for the future. The best course of action is not to consider what your neighbors have since it's unlikely that you know their entire situation much less there financial situation. My husband and I bought 1.5 acres for peace and quiet in a nice neighborhood. We built a house and shop that we could afford at the time without any credit on the farm side of the road. We didn't want to put tomorrow's money or credit in to the house at our age. Many of our neighbors have a river view and have larger homes that are expensive. I don't envy my investment in their house or their property tax bills. But I love our house decision because we have lots of room for cats to roam and the onion, potato, corn, and hay crops are beautiful to see. Instead, concentrate on your managing your finances with a balance of rationality and emotions to make the best decisions possible for you at that point in time.

The money choices we make daily, weekly, monthly, and annually are important because they affect our financial health, well-being, and social status. Adults have to decide what to do with their money whether they like it or not. Decisions are hard work, yet we make thousands of decisions in a lifetime about everything from what we are having for lunch to purchasing a vehicle and a home.

Money choices in our life are important because they narrow our unique needs and wants from endless possibilities regardless of how much money we have. Mark Cuban or Daymond John still make decisions on what to buy and invest in outside of Shark Tank. What we choose to do with our money during our lifetime is affected by our income, emotions, and values. It's important to not only explore how and what to do with our money but why we make the choices we do based upon our emotions and values.

As an individual, it's a challenge to figure out what we really want and make it fit with our financial situation-which is probably an understatement. In a relationship or family, communication and negotiation are essential to arrive at a consensus that fits the budget. When we think of money choices and decisions they seem simple, requiring either a yes or a no, but often they are more complex than that. It comes down to what we value in life, what works for us emotionally and rationally, and what can we have today versus tomorrow.

Today's world of instant gratification is buying it now regardless of whether or not it's in the budget or on credit. In paying for it with credit you may pay several times over for it over time. Merchants count on us to make impulse purchases since they reap the rewards on quick decisions so slow down to make sure your decision is the right one. There's a reason that there is financing available at car dealers on the weekends and it's not to your benefit. For big decisions, I usually sleep on it and wakeup the next morning with a better solution to a problem.

The psychologies behind the reasons we spend, save, and go into debt vary with each individual. Some decisions involve acquiring debt, which means they are decisions that will have consequences beyond today. Everyone is unique, so it's a question of what is the best financial choice for those individuals, given their options, at this point in time. Personal finance is like a puzzle in which we must fit all the information we have at a point in time into a competent decision. While hindsight is always 20/20, decisions are based upon an estimate of what we think will happen in the future. Unfortunately, no one has a crystal ball yet.

Financial Responsibility

Today, with financial resources and tools on the internet, society has a whole has opened up more about poor financial decisions and the repercussions. Personal Finance books, seminars and lectures are everywhere to get everyone to become financially responsible for their actions or choices.

Earning money is more difficult than taking care of it, but learning to be financially responsible is part of being an adult. Keep in mind that there are a lot of professionals such as bank representatives, pension administrators, accountants, and financial advisors available to provide help. Obtaining a loan approval to borrow an amount of money doesn't mean it's prudent to borrow all of it since it can be more difficult to pay back that much year after year.

Instead, figure out payments that make sense since it's a large decision that requires research and thinking. Investing is the other side of financial responsibility, and careful research and risk assessment are key ingredients. Don't count on anyone to manage your money. Instead, decide to learn to manage money and get better at it over time. Taking care of finances is a part of life that requires adult behavior to manage, plan and execute good decisions.

Money

Money is used as a measurement stick of success, although success has many definitions. In today's society, there's an emphasis on having a lot of material goods and usually the more, the better. Some adults feel pressure to keep up financially with their neighbors or friends, and most school aged kids become aware of their parents' financial status by the home, vehicles, and toys they have. Peer pressure to have the coolest clothes and cars in high school and beyond is as intense as ever. It's a dream for many to find instant wealth by getting on the right TV show or Internet venue, hoping for instant fame that bypasses hard work. It comes down to lifestyles and different levels of needs or money. Some people think money can buy happiness or contentment. It can to a certain extent, since money can buy time off and material items.

The bottom line is you have to consider what success looks like for you.

When we think of wealthy families such as Henry Ford and the Rockefeller a legacy of money may create higher expectations to manage the family fortune for the next generation but may not bring personal happiness. Some high earning celebrities and sports figures have spent a lot of money and damaged their financial future by having someone else manage their money rather than keeping a close watch on their assets.

Ground Zero

Most of us start off with very little money, but over time and through hard work and saving, we can manage to amass a small fortune. Some families consider money a secret and won't discuss it, while other parents are more open to talking to and teaching their children about saving and spending. Other individuals would rather talk about their sex lives than money. There is no doubt that money or lack or money is very important in our lives since it affects our lifestyle and social status as well as retirement.

Emotions

Emotions feeling that fluctuate Feelings do not happen in isolation and are responses to significant situations in an individual's life that may motivate actions. Childhood experiences with money, parental views and cultural attitudes have an extraordinary influence on our money choices since that is how we initially learn money habits that may not change. Most people have set their saving and spending habits for life and don't usually change much unless they are pressured in a situation or required to in a relationship. Since money is something needed in exchange for something we want, money can be a motivator. Unfortunately, a lack of money to cover needs usually causes negative emotions and anxiety, while an abundance of money can create positive emotions due to all the material goods, security and experiences it can buy.

Keep in mind that feelings can be contagious and have an impact on people around us at work and home. It's easy to pick up how some people are feeling when their feelings are apparent. Conversely, others are good at hiding their feelings. The transfer of emotions affects organizations, since everyone brings them to work and they affect performance as well as drive behaviors for better or worse. Our emotions affect our personal and professional relationships as well as our decisions. Usually a person's disposition is positive or negative and is apparent as you get to know that friend, co-worker or relative. Positive people tend to be better in the workplace because they cognitively process more efficiently and more appropriately as well as handle more information effectively.

I steer clear of people in a bad mood because their energies are going to a useless place. Negative people can suck the energy out of an idea or even an entire room. A good way to change moods is to take a break, walk around, and get a glass of water to drink. People are drawn to positive personalities so I try to avoid negative personalities that usually have perpetual problems. Personalities affect life and financial decisions, so it's good to know how to manage emotions when dealing with relationships and money.

The Emotional Brain

We know that we use our brains to think through decisions. However, most of us don't think of our brain as a muscle that weighs two to three pounds that we use every day. There are two sides to our brains.

The left or analytical -brain works with logic, numbers, and financial issues. The right or emotional brain is where pictures, stories and music reside.

Both sides of the brain work daily, and there's no switch to turn one side or the other side off for the day. Most of us don't think about exercising our brain like we exercise our body in the gym, but our brain does need exercise. Exercising a few times a week keeps the body in shape as well as helps with brain processes such as production of endorphins that give us a sense of well-being. Something that most people don't know is that the brain can become fitter and better organized much like our closets or storage shelves. In learning more about a subject, it becomes better connected and makes more sense as well as quicker to retrieve since its stored better. Other good ways to exercise the brain are by working on new tasks and learning new things.

The first lesson is about emotions and learning throughout life. As a student of life, we should recognize that emotions play a part in our financial decisions sometimes to our detriment. It's important to think through our money decisions rationally AND emotionally before making large life changing financial decisions.

Lesson 2 Personal Planning

The second lesson is about personal planning or applying business principles to your life. Organizations create strategic plans so why not apply strategic planning at the personal or individual level of an organization? There is a saying that if you have a plan chances are that you will end up where you want to be rather than by chance.

The purpose of personal strategic planning is to find direction, meaning, and purpose to life, make decisions that positively affect the future, and focus energies on what's most important. A plan helps achieve the greatest results in the shortest period of time. It also helps you enjoy more time, money, and balance, enhance your quality of life, and experience overall peace of mind. So why not work on your plan?

Gary Ryan Blar suggests the following for creating a personal strategic plan: "Personal strategic planning is based on the premise that life will not go according to plan, if you do not have a plan." A successful plan must include the following:

1. Personal Philosophy: Every person has a personal philosophy consisting of some rules adopted from one's parents, culture, religion, acquaintances, and other influences. A philosophy is defined as the most basic beliefs, concepts, and attitudes of an individual. In other words, it answers the question, "What is your approach to living your life?" To define your personal philosophy, answer five key questions:

1) What do you get up each and every morning wanting to do?

2) What directs your actions and decisions, especially the impulsive ones?

3) What gives you a sense of satisfaction at the end of the day?

4) Why are your beliefs important to you?

5) How does your philosophy measure up to higher standards or ideals? Thinking through these questions will enable you to define your personal philosophy. Don't make it complex; keep it simple. These answers aren't easy and I keep working on it.

2. Legacy Statement: Your legacy serves as your life's defining statement. It provides an overarching framework for all mission statements and goals to follow and answers the question, "What do I want to be remembered for?"

3. Mission Statement: A mission statement is a declaration of who you are, why you exist, and what you intend to accomplish. In personal planning, the question is, "What is my life's business and reason for being?" A personal mission statement is similar to a corporate mission statement, but it is individualistic. The main rule to follow when developing your personal mission statement is that if you are inspired by it, and if it captures the essence of how you want to live your life and project yourself, then it is good. Here is an example of a personal mission statement:

I will look for strengths in others, and the good in every situation.

I will live with an attitude of gratitude.

I will repay every kindness shown to me.

I will live, work, and play with renewed spirits.

That was fun and easy to let's move on to more topics.

4. Core Values: Our values act as our compass, guiding us through life's terrain. One certain way of knowing that you are living in accordance with your values is by defining guidelines.

5. Code of Ethics: A definition of a code of ethics is a sense of morality, both professionally and personally. Codes of conduct, personal creeds, and pledges all reflect an effort to make sense of things, to organize behavior, and to better understand ourselves. Ethics is a set of expectations for behavior that defines values in terms of morality and legality, both professionally and personally. Moral responsibility is a set of principles that provides a framework for making decisions individually and in a group. These written rules help define specific behaviors of a particular group of trades and professions such as accounting, law, and engineering to standardize good behaviors and prohibit or limit some actions. Both of my accounting credentials, CPA-Certified Public Accountant and CMA-Certified Management Accountant require on continuing professional education in ethics. Values and ethics are defined on an individual basis and should be congruent with workplace ethics. Over time, it becomes apparent whether or not the organization that you work for is a good fit of value. Ethics start at the individual level of every organization and we are all responsible for our individual behavior.

6. Lifetime Objectives: Your objectives should be written within the framework of your Legacy & Mission Statements. The key to any personal strategic plan is to visualize your desired outcomes in advance. Be sure to write and rewrite your lifetime objectives as affirmations of the future you are working to realize.

7. Goals: The key in writing your goals is to make them measurable, specific, and time-bound. Goals need to be written for each of the ten critical areas of life to include: Personal, Health, Recreation, Family, Friends, Community, Career, Financial, Household and Spiritual.

Lifetime Objectives and Goal Setting

Plan and set goals for savings and retirement, debt, and expenses using three time frames: short-term (one year), intermediate (one to five years), and long-term (five to ten years). Here are five golden rules of goal setting:

First, set goals that motivate you. When you set goals for yourself, it is important that they motivate you. This means making sure that they are important to you and that there is value in achieving them. Set a few goals that relate to the high priorities in your life. Weight loss is a common goal i.e. to fit a particular dress for a special event. Many of my goals have been to start and finish degrees and credentials which I always do since I have become pretty disciplined. Eventually I had to move my retirement goal up my ladder as I get older.

Second, set SMART goals.. The simple fact is that for goals to be powerful, they should be designed to be SMART: **S**pecific, **M**easurable, **A**ttainable, **R**elevant, and **T**ime-Bound.

Specific Goals-Your goal must be clear and well defined. Remember, you need goals to show you the way. Make it as easy as you can to get where you want to go by defining precisely where you want to end up.

Measurable Goals-Include precise amounts, dates, and other details in your goals so you can measure it.. If your goal is simply to reduce expenses, how will you know when you have been successful? Reduce expenses by a certain amount (e.g., $100 per month) or by a percentage so you can measure the goal from month to month. A college class grade is a measurable goal and so is weight lost. Pick a measure that works for you.

Attainable Goals-Make sure that it's possible to achieve the goals you set. If you set a goal that you have no hope of achieving, you will erode your confidence but resist the urge to set goals that are too easy. Set a goal and achieving it creates great personal satisfaction.

Time-Bound Goals-Your goals must have a deadline so that you know when you can celebrate success. When you are working on a deadline, your sense of urgency increases and achievement will come that much quicker. Make it a week, a month or up to a year keeping in mind that shorter goals are easier to accomplish.

Third, set goals in writing. The physical act of writing down a goal makes it real and tangible. As you write, use the word "will" instead of "would like to" or "might." Frame your goal statement positively and put them on the refrigerator or your bathroom mirror.

Fourth, make an action plan. This step is often missed in the process of goal setting. By writing out the individual steps, and then crossing each one off as you complete it, you'll realize that you are making progress towards your ultimate goal. This is especially important if your goal is big and demanding, or if it is geared toward a long-term outcome.

Fifth, stick with it! Remember, goal setting is an ongoing activity -- not just a means to an end. Build in reminders to keep yourself on track, and make regular time-slots available to review your goals. The process of goal setting often results in goal attainment so new goals can be set to reach. This is where so many people fail. Students stop coming to class because the content is boring or difficult to learn and it sets failure in motion.

Persistence is the key to everything-stick with it.

8. Personal Board of Directors: A personal board will accelerate your progress by providing both wisdom and support for the attainment of a specific purpose. Find some mentors to work within your company and or accomplished individuals that would like to mentor.

9. Maintenance & Performance Check-Ups: On a monthly or quarterly basis, you should pause to evaluate your performance, progress, and what can be done better.

10. Personal Reason Why: You won't become successful until and unless you identify, support and empower your reasons why. Your whys provide fuel for achievement and are the reasons

In the second lesson on personal planning, creating a plan is better than no plan at all. Even thinking about a plan is useful or better than no plan at all so use what you can to apply to your life. Set your goals, accomplish them, and set new bolder goals to move forward and be successful. This all sounds like a lot of work on you-yes it is but go for it since you are worth it. At this point in my life, I continue to write plans and set new goals that give me a purpose in life.

Lesson 3 Mindset for Success

Mindsets

The third lesson is about creating a successful mindset in life. A mindset is our mental attitude that has taken shape based on our life experiences, our environment, our education and the ideas and beliefs we have absorbed from those people we have interacted with the most in our lives. Our mindset is that inner conversation taking place in our heads. There are a lot of different approaches to mindsets covering many topics including abundance, attitudes of gratitude, creativity, growth, entrepreneurship, happiness, power, positive thinking, success, and time management. In choosing the success mindset, for example, having the correct mindset for a particular task is almost a prerequisite for success. No one has ever been successful who has not had to overcome hurdles and obstacles to that success. The ability to have an empowering and positive outlook and mindset allows us to not only overcome those hurdles and obstacles to success, but to actually welcome them as challenges and opportunities for growth and learning. Often people with very similar circumstances in life can bring about very different results, purely because of their mindset. Our mindset regarding certain situations and events influences our interpretation of them and often predetermines the way in which we respond. People with positive mindsets are able to overcome life's many setbacks far more easily than those with negative mindsets. It is our choice to live a life controlled by random thoughts or decide to choose our thoughts carefully and to develop a positive, empowering and successful mindset. No one else can make this mindset choice for you.

Where there is a will there is a way.

Fixed Versus Growth

Carol Dweck is a researcher at Stanford University well–known for her work on "the fixed mindset versus the growth mindset." In a fixed mindset, students believe their basic abilities, intelligence, and talents are just fixed traits. They have a certain amount and that's that; then, their goal becomes to look smart all the time and never look dumb. In a growth mindset, we understand our talents and abilities can be developed through effort, good teaching, and persistence. They don't necessarily think everyone's the same or anyone can be Einstein, but they believe everyone can get smarter if they work at it so let's get started NOW.

Other Mindsets

A banker's mindset has four components. First, borrow from yourself by turning debts into assets and creating real wealth in the process. Second, expect the unexpected and protect it through insurance. Third, leave a legacy rather than a tax burden. Fourth, create wealth by thinking like a banker. Rather than appearing before a banker, filling out the forms, and hoping for a loan, rethink your position and use a banker's mindset. Obviously, not everyone is in a financial position to have a banker's mindset, but it is possible if the wealth has been created.

Another mindset is those of poverty thinkers who focus on cutting costs and reducing involvement, which results in decreasing motivation and cash hoarding. They paralyze their decision-making process, hold back constantly, complain, and seek outside approval.

On the other hand, prosperity thinkers brainstorm ways to increase income, work on self-improvement, set attainable goals, and celebrate baby steps. They keep money moving, trust that crises equal opportunity, give gratitude, and build internal confidence.

Wealthy Mindsets

John Lowery wrote *Prosperity Mindset vs. Lack of Mindset* and notes the wealthy focus more on what they want and less on what they don't in contrast to the poor, who are always focused on more of what they don't want. Wealthy people think differently and worry less, while some of the hardest working people are still broke. One of the worst things that can be done is to always focus on getting out of debt since it's a negative word. Focus on the positive of wealth building and give your time rather than money. Spend as little time as possible with people who feel badly about money since that will sabotage your unconscious and make it more difficult to attract more money into your life. Instead, reprogram your brain to attract more abundance into your life. Sounds interesting but I challenge you to try it.

One of my passions is reading about is how to become wealthy and how individuals have done so. There are many types of mindsets ranging from negative to positive on a myriad of topics. Changing a mindset is possible with self-discipline and work but there are marketing forces working on us so keeping a positive mindset and an eye on our finances is critical.

Personalized Marketing

Marketing has evolved to be individualized through the collection of data collected by companies where we shop. Think about those rewards cards are collecting information about what we purchase and when. Consumer behavior is influenced by technologies, market research and strategies to get the consumer to want and purchase more. Marketing techniques are evolving as information is collected from consumers about their choices and preferences of food, clothing, and other purchases from big box stores. The data collection starts with preference cards and polls, resulting in more niche marketing and specialized coupons headed your way in social media and email. Marketing is becoming more personalized with Amazon's recommendations to bundle or purchase more of your products. Retailers continue to refine marketing with new forms of social media ranging from Twitter to Pinterest, Instagram, and others. Shopping on the Internet with a phone, computer or other technologies has become so convenient that it's easy to spend too much money. Retailers are reaching out more than ever to compete for those dollars using a variety of social media and preference cards to gather information on preferences and trends. The line between what we need and want is pretty fuzzy thanks to marketing.

Marketing is about creating needs that didn't exist in previously. Consumers have more information available to them than ever, allowing them to easily comparison shop on a tablet or mobile online or in the store. The consumer has become price conscious as well as quality savvy by reading the product and service reviews on the web.

Consumers have more information than ever available make good decisions and save time.

Needs

Needs are defined as goods or services that are required or basic. This would include needs for food, clothing, shelter and health care. Wants are goods or services that are not necessary but that we desire or wish for. For example, one needs clothes, but one may not need designer clothes. One needs food but does not have to have steak or dessert. In the area of technology, a computer may be required to complete school assignments at home rather than the library. However, there is a certain level of perceived expectation to keep up with society or to fit in that most people participate in such as getting a better phone, a larger television, or a faster computer. Technology is one area that changes so fast that every few years or sooner, something "should" be replaced to keep up with the trends and to fit in with friends and family. Needs and wants can become murky, but it comes down to budgeting and making good decisions.

Maslow's Hierarchy of Needs (1943) is taught in many management and psychology courses. The expanded eight-stage model of the hierarchy of needs was developed in the 1960s by Abraham Maslow. The levels are as follows:

1) Biological and Physiological needs, 2) Safety needs, 3) Belongingness and Love needs, 4) Esteem needs, 5) Cognitive needs, 6) Aesthetic needs, 7) Self-actualization and 8) Transcendence.

Psychologist Abraham Maslow Self-actualized people are those who are fulfilled and doing all of which they are capable. The specific form that these needs will take will of course vary greatly from person to person. In one individual it may take the form of the desire to be an ideal mother, in another it may be expressed athletically, and in still another it may be expressed in painting pictures or in inventions."

Most people confuse needs and wants since they think that what they want is a need. Once the basic needs are met -- biological and physiological, safety, belongingness and love -- it comes down to the question, "What do you really want?"

Wants

Judith Stephens of Financial Fitness suggests staying focused on your wants since thoughts don't simply reflect your current reality. "Your thoughts create your reality. Don't let your mind wander into the minefield of what you don't want. Don't go there. Pull your mind back, take control of your thoughts and think about what you want in your life." On the list of wants, most people want more of everything including better vacations, recreational vehicles, entertainment, clothes, personal care and other items. Most of us think we would like to be wealthy and have all of our wants met, which does sound good. It's human nature to always want more of something or the bigger, better, and super-sized version. As adults, once we are employed full-time, spending usually is commensurate with our incoming funds for forty or fifty years.

In retirement, spending or wants slow significantly and comes almost to a halt when people are 75 years or older. Many seniors stop replacing items and don't update much in the way of household furnishings. The material wants seem to almost disappear with advanced age as quickly as they appeared to working adults. Global travel becomes more difficult due to aging and health problems, so you don't see a lot of people in their 80s and 90s traveling extensively. The best time to travel is when you can afford the time and have the money.

In the third lesson, understanding mindsets and our wants and needs are important. The mindset that you decide upon can be changed but it's up to you to decide how your mindset affects your wants and needs and how you choose to live your life.

Life is a series of choices.

Lesson 4 Individual Attributes

In the fourth lesson, individual attributes are explored to get you thinking. You, as an individual, are on a journey of life equipped with a unique combination of experiences, genetics, strengths, energy, health, and happiness whose job it is to make good money choices for you and your family. You were born in to this world as an individual and will leave the world as an individual when you die with a lifespan up to 100 years. Our most productive working life lasts about 50 years, from our 20s to our 70s depending upon the individual. When you think about it, our time is limited to obtain many experiences and accomplishments within a lifetime. The money choices you make have more consequences than you realize because they affect others in positive and negative ways. It is your responsibility to take care of yourself first, similar to putting your oxygen mask on first in an airplane, so you can help take care of others. Keep in mind that you are the Chief Learning Officer (CLO) for you, so don't plan on anyone else assuming that role. As an individual with many good attributes, you are in charge of yourself and need to know yourself, invest in yourself and take care of yourself.

- The ways in which others (particularly significant others) react to us.

- How we think we compare to others (e.g., we feel positive about the self when we do better than our reference group).

- Our social roles (e.g., the role of doctor or celebrity may carry more prestige in contrast to roles associated with blue collar positions).

- The extent to which we identify with other people through roles and groups we belong to.

How we perceive ourselves or our self-concept is important because how we treat ourselves is how others will treat us. When we respect our self, then others will return the respect.

Intelligences

When we think of intelligence, the term IQ -- or Intelligence Quotient generally describes a score on a test that rates the subject's cognitive ability in comparison to the general population. A score between 90 and 100 indicates average intelligence while a score above 130 indicates exceptional intelligence. In addition to IQ, emotional Intelligence, or EI, has been a topic of discussion. The idea is to teach people how to be emotionally intelligent and how to manage the emotions of their employees. **Emotional intelligence is defined as the ability to understand and manage both your own emotions, and those of the people around you.** People with a high degree of emotional intelligence usually know what they're feeling, what this means, and how their emotions can affect other people.

Strengths

Most people jump to their weaknesses first and consider their strengths last. Most people concentrate on making their weaknesses stronger rather than making their strengths stronger.

Marcus Buckingham has written *The ONE thing you need to know, Go Put Your Strengths to work,* and *StandOut.* No one is good at everything, so delegate or partner on your weak areas. Marcus advocates thinking about our strengths and making them stronger, which makes so much sense because everyone is unique. A few examples of strengths are creativity, curiosity, open-mindedness, love of learning, bravery, persistence, integrity, vitality, love, kindness, gratitude, hope, humor, humility, fairness, forgiveness, and spirituality. Although this is not a complete list, it's important to identify and think about your strengths. There are several strengths and weaknesses tests, inventories, and surveys available on the Internet.

Boundaries

Knowing your strengths and your boundaries is important. There are two types of boundaries: emotional and physical. Healthy emotional boundaries include knowing when to say NO, valuing your self-esteem, being assertive, valuing your time, empowering yourself in a partnership, and taking care of your own needs. Physical boundaries include your body, your sense of personal space, sexual orientation and privacy. Other physical boundaries involve clothes, shelter, safety, money, information, space, noise, etc. It's important to know and set your boundaries because if you don't, no one else will. Setting and making known your boundaries reflects your self-esteem and self-confidence. People that you want in your life should have their own boundaries as well as respect your boundaries. Keep in mind a rule regarding time-sensitive information about opportunities and other confidential information -- don't share it if you aren't comfortable. Instead, tell the asking party to check with the original party about sharing the information. In general, it's best to under share than to give out too much information. If you aren't comfortable with a conversation, change the subject or leave. One aspect of emotional intelligence is sensing your peers' and boss's boundaries and respecting them.

Mindfulness

Mindfulness is found in Buddhist teachings and is often found in yoga and meditation techniques. In the October 2013 ***Mindful Magazine*** article, ***To Pause and Protect***, Maureen O'Hagan discussed how Oregon police officers are learning mindfulness techniques to deal with stress, be more focused on the job, and connect more meaningfully with the people they serve. The officers

engage in mindfulness meditation and classes to help

become more aware of stress and to mitigate its impact.

Some of the mindfulness language was customized to "pay

attention to what's happening around you. Notice the

thoughts." Practicing mindfulness is like building muscle

memory with the repetition. Mindfulness is where

emotional intelligence and wellness come together. Here

are some principles of mindfulness:

Do one thing at a time -- don't multi-task.

Do it slowly and deliberately, not rushed and randomly.

Do less -- prioritize and let go what isn't important.

Put space in your schedule for relaxation.

Spend five minutes each day doing nothing.

Focus on the present, and stop worrying about the future.

Within mindfulness, flow is characterized as the mental state of operation in which a person performing an activity is fully immersed in a feeling of energized focus, full involvement, and enjoyment in the process of the activity. In essence, flow is characterized by complete absorption in what one does. According to Csikszentmihalyi, flow is completely focused motivation. It is a single-minded immersion and represents perhaps the ultimate experience in harnessing the emotions in the service of performing and learning.

As an example, think about setting an hour or two a week for you to spend on a new project related to work such as reading about current trends, learning a new skill or immersing yourself in studying something. Find a quiet place for you to work and immerse yourself to let the time go by while you are in the flow. **Please check out mindfullness.org**

Happiness

Mark Lesser, a Zen priest, has 30 years of experience in thinking and teaching Zen life balance. His book, ***Z.B.A.: Zen of Business Administration***, is about his life as a monk and the creation of Brushdance, a recycled paper company. According to Mark the secrets of happiness include four items.

1) Self-esteem: Happy people like themselves.

2) Optimism: Happy people are hope-filled, are healthier, and enjoy greater success.

3) Extroversion: Happy people are outgoing, self-assured, and confident that others will like them.

4) Personal control: Happy people believe they choose their destinies and make decisions that affect their future.

In keeping with the secrets of happiness let's move on to positive thinking.

Mindfulness, happiness and positive thinking accompany success.

Positive Thinking

The positive thinking movement emerged from the field of psychology in recent years. In the past, the focus of psychology was to concentrate on diagnosing and improving bad behaviors. Positive thinking is a mental attitude that sees the bright side of things and anticipates happiness, joy, health, and favorable results. Mindsets, happiness, mindfulness, and positive thinking have synergies and work together. If you adopt this mental attitude, you teach your mind to expect success, growth and favorable outcomes. In order to turn the mind toward the positive, some inner work is required, since attitude and thoughts do not change overnight.

To be successful:

1. Read about this subject, think about its benefits, and persuade yourself to try it. The power of your thoughts is a mighty power that is always shaping your life. This shaping is usually done subconsciously, but it is possible to make the process a conscious one. Even if the idea seems strange, give it a try. You have nothing to lose, but plenty to gain.

2. Ignore what other people say or think about you if they discover that you are changing the way you think.

3. Use your imagination to visualize only favorable and beneficial situations.

4. Use positive words in your inner dialogues, or when talking with others.

5. Smile a little more, as this helps to think positively.

6. Once a negative thought enters your mind, you have to be aware of it and endeavor to replace it with constructive thoughts.

7. It doesn't matter what your circumstances are at the present moment. Think positively, expect only favorable results and situations, and circumstances will change accordingly. If you persevere, you will transform the way your mind thinks.

8. Another useful technique is the repetition of affirmations. This technique is similar to creative visualization, and can be used together with it.

Start noticing the type of company you are keeping as friends and in the workplace. People are more disposed to help us if we are positive, and they dislike and avoid anyone broadcasting negativity. All of us affect and are affected by the people we meet, for better or worse. This happens instinctively and on a subconscious level through our words, thoughts and feelings, and body language.

In the fourth lesson remember positivity attracts positivity, both personally and professionally.

Lesson 5 Relationships

In the fifth lesson, relationships and finances are explored. Relationships are complex because they are several levels deep and always need work. They are easy to get in to and usually more difficult to get out of especially if marriage, children or assets are involved. Trust, respect, and willingness to work with a partner are some of the key ingredients of successful relationships. Add finances to relationships and it becomes more complicated and interesting. It's critical to work on keeping the relationship going in a positive direction and to spend time together. Managing finances and the relationship are challenges in life; in fact, wedding vows should probably be updated to include "until debt do we part" rather than "until death do we part." Both parties should plan on giving time, respect, and love to make a relationship and/or marriage work. A good rule to follow is what you give in a relationship, you receive in return. Marriage is a partnership that should involve friendship and love as well as caring and an interdependence over the years.

Keep in mind that what you have to offer is what you may get in a mirror image.

If you are good with money, that is what you also want; if you aren't good with money, you should be because that could open the door to scams, con artists, or someone who wants your credit. Find out if you are financially compatible before you think about marriage, or live together and see how that works out financially.

Although money is one of the leading causes of break-ups and divorce, many couples don't discuss finances and spending before they get married, reports Forbes.com. They don't realize that marriage is a partnership through good and bad times or for better or worse, as stated in many wedding vows. A factor contributing to the lack of communication about finances is the rising trend of both individuals living at home, with Mom and Dad, with no clue about what it's going to cost to operate a household.

Melissa Leong of *Young Money* notes, "Financial conflict is stronger, longer lasting and predicts divorce better than other marital issues." Arguments appear to be about dollars and cents, but they're really about power, commitment, ego, respect, and fairness. This generation of couples faces an added challenge as 30% of women now out-earn their spouses. According to research by Jeffrey Dew, an assistant professor at Utah State University, who studies families and financial strife, couples who disagreed about finances once a week were 30% more likely to split up than couples who said they argued about finances a few times a month. Dr. Dew also measured the link between consumer debt and a couple's likelihood for divorce.

"Every 10 fold increase in consumer debt was associated with a 7% increase in the likelihood of divorce. So people who had $1,000 of debt versus $100 would be 7% more likely to divorce." That's some strong evidence to take care of finances in relationships.

It's unfortunate because if couples divorce later and have purchased assets throughout the marriage, there will be a lot of communication about the division of assets, probably through attorneys. Divorce can very expensive if one spouse has to split a pension or a large asset such as an inheritance they brought to the marriage. The receiving spouse in essence gets a payout from the other spouse when assets are divided equally. That payout may result in the asset being sold to even out or distribute the assets. With the demand for divorces, attorneys specializing in divorce are busy too!

Spenders and Savers

Savers love to hold on to their money. They tend to be very organized with their finances, often having a clear, written budget and always knowing how much money is in their bank account. Savers watch their spending carefully, often to the point where they have a hard time justifying purchases that seem "frivolous" such as vacations or entertainment. Many savers worry about their future financial security and tend to be very conservative with where they choose to put their money. Savers often prefer the safety of a high interest savings account over investments such as mutual funds or stocks. That describes me and my husband so we are two savers so we won't argue much over money-just using it.

In contrast, spenders love to spend their money. They like the immediate pleasure that comes from buying things for themselves and from picking up the tab for dinner or buying gifts "just because." Spending money to accumulate "stuff" or to indulge themselves makes spenders happy, but they may also have a hard time prioritizing their spending and putting money aside for savings. Spenders tend to focus on living in the moment rather than looking at the bigger financial picture, and they often find themselves in debt because of their spending

Melissa Leong of Young Money suggests that we tend to marry our financial opposite. Spendthrifts marry tightwads. Spendthrifts admire savers for their discipline and stability while tightwads find spenders exciting. "There's value in both perspectives," says Toronto therapist Amanda Mills. "In a family, the spender is usually motivated by creating better quality of life in the present and the saver is motivated by causing better quality of life in the future. So they each have a place."

On Your Own

In the article ***Mine, Yours, and Ours***, Suze Orman discusses five Tips for women on mixing money and love.

She advocates that every woman needs her own savings in addition to a shared or joint account. The difference left over at the end of each month after household expenses are paid should be split, even though there may be only one income.

On a second note, every woman also needs one credit card in her name only should they become divorced.

Third, debts prior to marriage are yours alone and shouldn't be merged although both could pay on them.

Fourth, be pragmatic about the assets you bring into a marriage, such as inheritances, by working with an attorney.

Fifth, after you marry, every asset either of you acquires is jointly held, and long-term goals should be agreed upon together. This advice is good for men or women, and it's part of thinking through your finances. Talking to your partner about money is important whether you have similar or different spending and saving styles. Here are four crucial financial issues to discuss:

1) **Relationship goals**: Work out your relationship goals with your partner. Their background and experiences will influence how they think about money. Once you understand how your partner approaches financial matters, it will make it easier to create a money plan that suits you both.

2) **Current financial situation:** Take stock of all your earnings, savings, assets (any shares or property you own) and credit card debts and loans. Next, look at what goals you share: do you want to get married, buy a home or have a baby? Once you know, a joint budget will help you achieve these goals.

3) **Attitudes toward spending and saving**: Are you a spender or saver? How about your partner? Try to find common ground; work out what you can both afford.

4) **The financial controller:** Who will handle the finances? Will one person look after household expenses and the other the mortgage? Make sure you're both happy with the decision.

A few housekeeping items include putting both of your names on services like electricity, gas, phone and Internet. If both of your names are on the bill, then it's your shared responsibility. Make sure joint assets like your home are purchased in both your names, and that joint debts are in both names, not just one.

Financial Intimacy

Financial intimacy " is the ability to openly express your wants, needs, and desires in a clear and effective manner and to feel completely safe and vulnerable knowing that your partner can hold that for you," according to Deborah Price, author of *The Heart of Money: A Couple's Guide to Creating True Financial Intimacy.* The most common problem couples have is the inability to communicate about money effectively and in a healthy way. In working through the communication issues, it's important to identify the unconscious patterns that you accidentally inherited from your parents. The next step is to co-create a true alignment of the vision by communicating your hopes, dreams, and desires in order to focus on building a future.

Communication

Communication and negotiation are important to establishing and maintaining a financial system that works for couples. Dealing with money issues from the past as well as current and future expenses are challenging for everyone. The crux of money problems is lack of communication. Money is powerful and is a way to gain and stay in control since there may be differences in levels of responsibility in the relationship.

The first important thing to remember about communication in marriage is to consistently use "I" statements as opposed to starting out a sentence with the word "you." When beginning a sentence with "I," "I think," or "I feel," it's all about you and your feelings instead of placing blame, whether real or perceived, on the other person.

To achieve true communication in marriage, both spouses must make a **commitment to say what they mean, and mean what they say**. Many people, often without being aware, make a statement that says one thing, while their facial expression says the exact opposite. This forces the other partner to decide which one to react to and which one is more accurate, thus losing sight of the real matter at hand.

Set a good time

Yet another important thing to remember for healthy communication in marriage is to never discuss anything of importance when either one of you is angry, upset, or feeling tense. If both people are in a relaxed state, they're better able to get their feelings across without sounding accusatory or placing blame.

Marital communication is the strongest deterrent to divorce and is a factor that contributes to happiness and longevity of a marriage. Nonverbal cues have an effect on interpersonal exchanges, so partners should make an effort to be mindful of their tones, actions, attitudes, and the level of attention given to their partner. A closeness can be developed through frequent eye contact, open positioning of arms and legs, touching, and maintaining appropriate distance while communicating have all been found to contribute to marital satisfaction. Electronic communication can be a great way for couples to stay in touch when apart but should never serve as a substitute for face-to-face interaction when available. Married persons should never expose their secrets or vent anger towards their spouse online because it becomes public. Instead, work on improving communication at home throughout the day.

Common Goal

Remind yourselves of the importance of love, harmony, and unity between you and your partner. Focus on a common goal and agree on the problem or issue rather than trying to solve multiple problems at once. Once you have expressed your thoughts and feelings, visualize them going into a central discussion "pot." This allows the discussion to flow freely without either of you holding on to what you said. Encourage and freely share thoughts, feelings, and opinions with love, respect, and kindness. Carefully monitor and modify your attitude and tone of voice; if underneath your words is criticism, disrespect, or sarcasm, your spouse will hear this, even when your words are positive. Listen to each other carefully and without interruption and request clarification as needed. However, avoid deferring regularly rather than taking the time to thoroughly discuss an issue. Thorough discussions usually result in better and more creative solutions. Review significant decisions after some time trying them out to assess whether they are working or whether you need to change direction.

Negotiation

Some things can't be negotiated such as core values, integrity, spirituality, feelings and attitudes. The term negotiation is most popular in salary negotiations in business. However, negotiation is a crucial part of marriage and there are times when marriage is more important than careers and other activities. There are three common negotiating mistakes couples make:

1. Failure to prepare before negotiation with your partner,

2. Caving in too quickly to avoid tension,

3. Pushing your own solution.

Couples negotiation is more risky than business negotiation because more self-disclosure and emotional risk are involved. The consequences of negotiating affect you when deciding where to live and how to manage finances. In essence, the only things you can really negotiate are behavior and decisions.

In the fifth lesson, relationships change when it comes down to money. Communication and negotiation are the essential tools to better a relationship since many breakups occur due to different financial habits of spending and saving.

Lesson 6 Financial Statements

The sixth lesson is about basic personal financial statements. For individuals, there are two important statements: an income statement and a balance sheet although a budget is also important. We are going to look at the income statement and budget now with the balance sheet later in the chapter. An income statement, details income or money coming in and money going out for expenses and the difference or profit for a period of time (i.e., a month, quarter or year). Individuals want their income to be more than their expenses so the "extra" money can be moved to savings or used other months when there might be a deficit or when expenses are more than income.

Budget

A budget is similar to an income statement because compares an estimate or your goals of income and expenses to actual income and expenses for a period of time, usually for a month and up to a year. In the budget, a column for the difference or variance can be calculated that is positive or negative helping you understand if more was saved more than anticipated or budgeted or more spent more than planned. It's definitely work creating and keeping up a budget in a spreadsheet if you are on a tight budget to see where money is going. Budgets are useful when they are customized to fit your needs, including debt payments and savings. Most importantly, control your spending and keep an eye on increasing income. Sitting down and figuring out your financial situation is important because in today's world, we must think further ahead than simply checking a bank balance every day. The biggest problem is LIVING WITHIN YOUR MEANS. If you live outside your means, then you are borrowing money from your future; worse yet, you are begging from others -- which could include the bank of Mom and Dad. If you're spending more than you are making, it will catch up with you and it can be difficult to pay it back in the future.

Expense Types

Fixed expenses are those that stay the same for periods of time such as mortgage payments or rent, and some utilities that are the same amount each month (e.g., Internet). Variable expenses vary with volume that is, the more that is used, the higher the bill will be. Examples of variable expenses are utilities, gas, groceries and other consumption items. Choose a fixed and variable budget or a traditional expense budget depending on which you find more useful to you. Find a software program or create your own budget in a spreadsheet and have fun with making graphs that help you make better decisions.

Diane Cook's Budget, is example of fixed and variable expenses used in a budget. In this scenario, there is extra money left over every month which is allocated to retirement, vacation, special savings and another category titled other which can be used for additional expenses.

DIANE COOK'S BUDGET

Janurary- June 30

Gross Annual $95,000

TAKE HOME INCOME	JAN	FEB	MAR	APRIL	MAY	JUNE	TOTAL
(after taxes)							
Salary	5,500	5,500	5,500	5,500	5,500	5,500	33,000
Wages		1,000	750	600	500	500	3,350
Interest Earned	5	5	6	6	7	7	36
Total Income	5,505	6,505	6,256	6,106	6,007	6,007	36,386
EXPENSES/Fixed							
Mortgage	1,635	1,635	1,635	1,635	1,635	1,635	9,810
Auto Loan	330	330	330	330	330	330	1,980
Credit Cards	200	200	200	200	200	200	1,200
Student Loans	380	380	380	380	380	380	2,280
Auto Insurance	108	108	108	108	108	108	648
Utilities	180	180	180	180	180	180	1,080
Total fixed exp.	2,833	2,833	2,833	2,833	2,833	2,833	16,998
EXPENSES/Variable							
Gas/Diesel	250	300	375	360	380	400	2,065
Groceries	415	435	450	445	495	500	2,740
Entertain/Eating Out	350	300	325	330	360	310	1,975
Health/Medical	250	300	350	325	330	375	1,930
Clothing	250	275	200	100	300	200	1,325
Personal/Misc.	200	250	225	275	240	200	1,390
Total variable	1,715	1,860	1,925	1,835	2,105	1,985	11,425
RECAP							
Total Income	5,505	6,505	6,256	6,106	6,007	6,007	36,386
Total fixed exp.	2,833	2,833	2,833	2,833	2,833	2,833	16,998
Total variable	1,715	1,860	1,925	1,835	2,105	1,985	11,425
Difference	957	1,812	1,498	1,438	1,069	1,189	7,963
Discretionary							
Retirement	500	500	500	500	500	500	3,000
Vacation	400	400	400	400	400	400	2,400
Special Savings	50	150	150	150	150	150	800
Other expenses	7	762	448	388	19	139	1,763

The second financial statement calculated is a balance sheet or a personal net worth statement that is for a specific date.

Assets

So let's start with basic definitions in a balance sheet. **Assets are described as resources you own whether they are paid for or owed for**. Examples of assets are cash, savings, vehicles, recreational vehicles, residence or home, rentals, stocks, bonds, mutual funds, pension funds and other types of investments.

Liabilities

Liabilities are anything owed such as vehicle loans, student loans, mortgage loans, and other loans.

Net Worth

Net worth or capital is the difference between assets and liabilities ow how much of the assets are owned by you instead of a bank or credit card. The balance sheet or net worth statement everyone should calculate annually to see what assets you own, owe on and their share of the assets or net worth. By looking at your liabilities, you can figure how much you owe and how long it will take you to get your liabilities to zero. So open a spreadsheet and create your own spreadsheet file with different sheets to track your situation over time.

Loan applications are the equivalent of net worth statements since lending institutions want to verify your assets and liabilities before making a loan to make sure that your assets are not overstated and liabilities aren't understated or not listed.

A good net worth statement to retire with is where your assets equal net worth and there is no debt; this way, income is only needed to pay current living expenses. Everyone wants a positive net worth and to own assets outright eventually. Diane Cook's Net Worth Statement is an example of an "average" net worth statement which is

on the next page.

DIANE COOK'S PERSONAL NET WORTH STATEMENT

As of June 30

ASSETS (What you own)	
Cash	350
Checking accounts	1,250
Savings acccounts/CDs	22,121
Market value of investments	18,678
Vehicles	14,500
Furniture and appliances	10,000
Technology	2,500
Clothing	2,850
Home	250,000
Pension	10,112
Other assets	1,200
TOTAL ASSETS	**333,561**
LIABILITIES (WHAT YOU OWE)	
Credit cards	12,211
Student Loans	18,300
Vehicle Loans	10,565
Other liabilities	1,000
Home Mortgage	198,000
Total Liabilities or debt	**240,076**
Assets-Liablities=Net Worth	
NET WORTH	**93,485**
TOTAL LIABILITIES NET WORTH	**333,561**

Increasing Net Worth

To increase your net worth, purchase more assets over time and make the assets you have more productive by finding better returns. Do this by reading and learning more about investments on the Internet or working with a financial advisor.

Another way to increase net worth is to decrease the liabilities you owe and make the liabilities cost less over time by finding better financing such as a fixed rate home-equity loan or pension loan. Finally, minimizing unnecessary expenses requires work (e.g., preparing food instead of eating out), since it takes discipline and motivation to increase net worth at any age.

Usually, two can live cheaper than one. Sharing rent or a mortgage usually results in a higher standard of living than going it alone. If you are in your 20s, 30s, 40s, 50s, or 60s your net worth statement or balance sheet may start out at zero or possibly negative. Net worth should increase with age so there are assets accumulated for retirement.

High net worth individuals have several characteristics in common: they have a positive attitude, are confident, manage their time very well, set goals, achieve them, and set new goals. They seek promotions and take on new challenges, are physically fit, and have above average intelligence. High net worth individuals create several income streams from different opportunities rather than rely on only one income.

Another strategy is to generate two incomes and choose to live on one income so the second income can be saved. Living on one income and saving the other gives financial flexibility to the partners should something happen to one of the jobs and helps build net worth quickly. There is no doubt that it's easier to accumulate net worth when there are two savers with incomes than when there is a single individual since there are some synergies in housing and

Other ways to increase net worth is to open or start a pre-tax account by checking with your human resources department to determine what programs are available. Increase your pre-tax retirement contributions including raises and bonuses that you can save every paycheck over the years. Before you know it, the contributions are at a maximum level. For after-tax money, start funding a Roth IRA from every paycheck and increase the amount you save every year, keeping in mind there are income limits that vary with the IRS tax code.

Decreasing Net Worth

Debt is a drag on your net worth since your money is used to pay loans consisting of principal and interest rather than increasing your net worth. Keep in mind inflation has averaged about three percent a year over the decades, and it will impact retirement funds for 20 to 30 years or more. Unfortunately, it's possible to have a negative worth if a home mortgage is more than the value of the home or if a vehicle is financed for more than seven years. Another item not shown on a net worth statement under assets is education (e.g., college degrees). Quite often student loans, a liability, take years to pay back, so a negative net worth can occur with student loans. Furthermore, net worth is decreased is through home equity loans by borrowing the equity built up in your home and not paying it back. The same situation can occur by borrowing from a pension loan and not repaying the loan. Finally, people panic when the stock market is low and selling investments when the price is low is a sure way to decrease worth since a loss on that investment is permanent. Instead, hang on to those stocks and a low market should be viewed as an opportunity to purchase stock at bargain prices.

Planning ahead and knowing your net worth is helpful for a good retirement and building wealth. Control your life and finances through good sense, self-control, and personal planning. There are five essential steps:

1) Assess your financial condition by using an income statement and balance sheet.

2) Implement a budget to rein in spending and plan for large purchases.

3) Develop a savings strategy to increase your net worth.

4) Pay off debt to increase your net worth.

5) Develop an investment plan to increase your net worth.

Net worth is what you have saved all your life, including the house you live in and your pension. The number serves as a guideline to help you figure out how much in assets you need to live off of in retirement and possibly pass on to another generation or entity, depending on your values. The sixth lesson is about financial statements and next worth. A question that you should ask yourself is where do you want to be in 10 years financially?

Lesson 7 Money Rules

The seventh lesson is on different money rules. Playing the game of Monopoly lasts a few hours, with money coming in from rents and other sources as well as going out to purchase properties and pay for expenses. As a kid, it's a good way to learn about a series of opportunities and how to make decisions. If you win at the game of Monopoly, you have accumulated a lot of money and someone else has gone broke or can't continue playing. In life, some of these circumstances are similar, but most people don't get rich in a few hours. Knowing financial rules can help you in the short-term and long-term by knowing more about assets and about how to manage your money better. A variety of money rules provide us guidance on how to make decisions that will help us get in to the normal range of financial activity. As with any guidelines or rules of thumb, there are always exceptions –

this is especially true in financial situations.

Rule 1 Organize

The first rule is to organize your financial papers,

financial statements, and tax returns. Start with good habits

by dealing with financial letters, bills, and correspondence

right away rather than tucking them into a drawer or worse

yet not opening the mail. Be sure to set up bill paying days

so you don't end up with a late charge that you could have

saved yourself. Most people keep copies of bills they really

don't need because if you need a copy of a bill, the

company has it. Utility, technology, and medical bills are

examples of personal bills that don't need to be saved

unless there's a good personal or business reason.

There are plenty of ways to organize your finances,

such as physically in boxes and on the computer. It's a

question of what works best for you to organize, track, and

analyze your finances every week, month, quarter, and year in various categories. The key to an organized life is to consistently stay on top of good habits and not get overwhelmed by putting things off and letting the papers or bills pile up. If you do a little work on your finances every few days, it doesn't turn into a large job.

Purchase a fireproof box for copies of all important documents: titles, passports, birth certificates, marriage certificates, pension plans and a list of all assets you own (e.g., valuables). Keep receipts of all appliances with model numbers to find replacement parts on the Internet. All insurance policies and their deductibles should be readily available in case of accidents (e.g., car accident, fire, fallen tree, broken window). File these documents in a timely manner.

Rule 2 Review

Review your checking account weekly, investment statements quarterly, and insurances, cable, and cell phone records annually to make sure you are getting the best deals. Another rule is to create your own deadlines that correspond with your paycheck and work schedule to stay on top of your finances; for example, you might check your account on a specific day or evening of the week. Fridays are good for some individuals since they correspond with paydays and it's a way to wrap up the week and review accounts. Stay consistent by using automatic payments for savings deposits and bill payments.

Rule 3 Daily Management

Managing your daily, weekly, or monthly cash requires figuring out how much you can spend daily on food, drinks such as energy, lattes or beer, gas, parking, and other expenses. If you overspend one day, then the next day you will have to underspend or cut back on another expense. Everyone has to manage his or her cash, so it's not a question of being rich or poor. Instead, it's learning to manage your money. Most wealthy people that earned their money manage their cash carefully since it's one of many money choices that we all have to make.

Individuals who pay on credit means they need to manage their future cash to pay for credit purchases today. If you have a very tight budget, then don't use much credit except to build up a credit score because it takes more effort to manage. If you charge or use credit for something, take the money and put it away in a drawer or earmark it to pay the future credit card bill or better yet pay the bill ahead. It's poor cash management to get in to the cycle of owing minimum payments on credit cards because it means paying for the item many times over since credit cards have a high interest rate.

Rule 4 Banking

Some people don't use a bank and instead pay check cashing fees which are expensive and a poor use of money. A second expense is the need for cashier checks to pay bills instead of using online banking, which is generally free. It's very expensive not to use a bank and to pay for those services separately. Using a bank requires managing cash and keeping a balance so there are no overdraft fees; however, many banks don't charge service fees anymore with a minimum balance, so this is a good place to stash some cash. Debit cards are very popular to use for purchases. This is one way to manage cash as long as you have enough money in your account so you don't incur overdraft fees, which can range from $25-40. If you accidentally incur a fee and you've only incurred one fee within a year, call the bank and ask to have the fee removed from your account. It doesn't hurt to ask, and the bank will often comply if you've been a good customer. It's often worth your time to get that money back. Another bank service that is usually free is online banking. This can be used to pay most bills on set dates, saving you time and stamps. Finally, many companies will automatically withdraw the amount owed monthly from your checking for free on a set date. Debit cards, online banking, and automatic payments are easy to set up at a bank or credit union, and they can save you time and money if you manage the incoming funds with the outgoing funds. There's also a record of payments and checks, which comes in handy if there is a payment dispute.

Rule 5 Know Your Numbers

Learning how much comes in from your paychecks and how much goes out monthly is a must for everyone. Take those monthly numbers and multiply them by 12 to look at them from an annual point of view. How much money you have AFTER paying the bills monthly or annually is something you should know. Most people realize they should be saving more money for retirement, replacements for vehicles, college tuition and expenses, replacements for household items, landscaping, and renovations. Most people would like to do more fun things but are limited by money choices. It's important to know what money is coming in to the household that meets needs and what is available for wants.

Rule 6 Furniture

Now let's look at rules for assets, starting with household furniture. NEVER EVER rent furniture. Instead, make do with gently used furniture from Craigslist, from relatives or friends. Do NOT finance furniture if you don't have the cash because this means you can't afford it. Save your money and purchase it in the future. Don't purchase furniture and plan to pay for it in four or five years because you may not have the money then and the furniture store is counting on you to pay for it with interest. By then your assets -- mattress, couch, or table – may be pretty worn out.

If you can't afford it today, buy used or save to purchase it later.

Maintenance agreements on appliances are available in the first year or two, but it's a personal preference. Keep in mind the value of your household assets is market value, or what they can be sold for, which is very different than the price you paid for them. Keep in mind that appliances depreciate over time rather than appreciate so they are not investments but expenses..

Rule 7 Vehicles

Over our lifetime, we purchase several vehicles and some recreational vehicles. Some individuals trade their vehicle in every couple of years for a new one and some of us drive it until the repairs exceed the value. A rule is to repair the vehicle if it's less than half of the trade. If more, sell it and purchase another vehicle. Some financial experts recommend never buy a new car until you are a millionaire, which usually doesn't happen for a while. Buy used because the depreciation is too large on a new vehicle, and buy the cheapest car your ego can afford.

The reality today is that the majority of vehicles are purchased with secured loans and most households have some type of vehicle payment. Keep in mind the value of your vehicles is the corresponding number in the Blue Book or what they can be sold for, which is very different than the price you paid for them. As a final rule, drive your method of transportation for ten years or more to get your money out of it.

Rule 8 Technology& Clothing

The value of both technology and clothing drops drastically after you purchase them. Most people purchase their technology new since it becomes obsolete so fast. New clothing becomes Goodwill value once it's used, so there is very little value in these items.

An asset or investment is good for more than one year, while an expense is used up in less than a year, so one can argue that coats, suits, and shoes are good for more than a year and may be a good investment. The ways of the past of saving up for an item are largely gone, although layaway is making a comeback with some retailers. The advantage of layaway is that the retailer lays the merchandise away so it is essentially sold until all payments are made. This eliminates the risk of no payment so the consumer doesn't have to pay interest on the item.

Rule 9-Housing

Some individuals own a residence and a vacation home, which may be a rental. **Though a mortgage should be no more than 28% of gross income,** there's no rule that can be found on what percentage of home(s) should be of net worth. My best guess is 20%-40% of net worth could be used on housing/vacation homes depending upon the situation. There are exceptions, such as Warren Buffet, who lives in a small home in Omaha, Nebraska. His home would be a fraction of his net worth even after giving much of his wealth to the Gates Foundation.

Rule 10 Investments

My best advice is don't invest in anything you don't understand, and don't let anyone pressure you into a quick decision about buying something. There are many types of investments ranging from real estate to the stock market so get educated before you make a decision. If you decide to purchase land or a building, get an inspector and don't take your broker's word for it.

Short Rules

Rule of 10: To gain perspective on potentially big purchases, think about how you will feel about the purchase in 10 days, 10 weeks and 10 years. For example, when thinking about a luxury car: In 10 days, I'll still be excited about the new car smell and it's a nice ride. In 10 weeks, it's just the machine I use to get to work and the supermarket. In 10 years, I'll barely remember this car.

Day-per-hundred rule: For a pricey discretionary item, give yourself time to cool off. Wait one day for every $100 the thing costs. If you still want it at the end of that time, consider buying it.

Savings: Save 10 percent of your take-home pay and it should be on top of retirement savings, so the total may be 20% or more.

Big ticket items: Funerals and weddings are where emotions and money come together. Do some planning to limit the expenditures before the events.

Debit and credit cards: Debit cards take money out of the account immediately, so check the balance before making a purchase. Credit cards require management of your money tomorrow but the rewards, depending on the card, do add up, so it works well to charge most items, including groceries, to maximize the rewards amount. It depends on your financial situation and what works for you. Credit cards may be used frequently to maximize rewards and minimize check writing and debit card usage.

Total debt: Total monthly debt payments should not exceed 36 percent of your gross monthly income. Pay debts from highest interest rate to lowest or from the smallest amount to the largest to reduce the debt the fastest and make it easier to handle as well as give you a sense of making good progress.

Home equity loans: Home equity loans should be paid back and shouldn't be used for vacations or small expenses. Home equity is similar to a savings account and should be left alone as an investment for the future.

Holiday spending: Spend no more than 1.5 percent of your gross income on the holidays, including gifts, decorations and travel.

Charitable gifts: Give only to tax-deductible charities. Do not give to individuals since those donations are not deductible. Most families have someone who can't manage his or her money and always has problems, but giving them money won't solve the problem.

Life insurance: Buy a policy worth six to ten times your gross annual income when you have to support children. Review your policy and needs when the children have moved out and are working.

College borrowing: Don't borrow more money than you'll make in your first year working after graduation. Don't work on a second degree full-time unless you know where there's a job.

Rent college textbooks: Typically, they rent for 1/3 of the cost, which may be cheaper than purchasing a used book with no resale if a new edition is coming out.

Double income: Some argue that when two individuals are working, the taxes are too high because the second income is added on top of the first income and the net gain is marginal. Maximizing pre-tax deductions to reduce taxable income is a great way to reduce taxes both paychecks and. save money. I gradually increased the amounts going to pre-tax over the years until we are at the limit.

Keep in mind that it's easier to grow pre-tax money than after-tax money.

Many people don't consider that extra income can go a long way toward debt reduction or savings. The total package may include a pension and other small benefits such as discounts, food on the job, a clothing allowance, or other perks. In today's world of divorce, that second job may become sole support for a household or provide enough experience to gain better employment. I believe that marriage is a partner and both individuals need to work and appreciate the value of money and a career.

Recommended Percentages of Gross Income:

1/4 on housing -- 25%

1/6 on transportation -- 13%

1/10 on food -- 10%

1/10 on savings (range should be from 10-30%)

1/25 on entertainment -- 4%

1/33 on clothes -- 3%

Housing, transportation, and savings -- 25%, 13%, and 10-30% -- are the largest items in a budget, depending on how much is saved. Keep in mind this is after-tax money and that taxes took a portion of your paycheck. There are some exceptions. For instance, if a house is paid for, then the number drops, but taxes and maintenance still need to be paid for.

The seventh lesson is on money rules, ten major rules plus quick rules and percentages or rules of thumb to use. Refer back to the rules when thinking through financial decisions.

Lesson 8 Pets and Wellbeing

The eighth lesson is on furry friends and wellbeing which are very important topics. The Humane Society of the United States article, *Pets by the Numbers,* notes the U.S. has come a long way over the last few decades in increasing pet ownership and decreasing euthanasia. From 1970 to 2010, the number of dogs and cats in homes has increased from 67 million to 164 million. However, there's still work to do: An estimated 2.7 million healthy shelter pets are not adopted each year, and only about 30 percent of pets in homes come from shelters and rescues.

Here are a few numbers of interest regarding dogs:

78.2 million - Number of owned dogs in the U.S.

46 percent - Percentage of U.S. households that own at least one dog

60 percent - Percentage of owners with one dog

28 percent - Percentage of owners with two dogs

$248 - Average annual amount spent by dog owners on routine veterinary visits

For comparison, here are some statistics about cats:

86.4 million - Number of owned cats in the U.S.

39 percent - Number of U.S. households that own at least one cat

52 percent - Percentage of owners with more than one cat

2.2 - Average number of owned cats per household

$219 - Average annual amount spent by cat owners on routine veterinary visits

The Utah Animal-Assisted Therapy Association defines pet therapy as the use of animals to promote health and healing. This therapy can be used with persons of any age, from children to senior citizens, and the benefits can be physical, mental and emotional. Research has shown that petting animals can bring down a person's blood pressure and trigger the release of dopamine and serotonin in the brain, which can elevate mood. Pet therapy can help lower stress, blood pressure, dementia symptoms, and other problems. Although dogs and cats are the animals most commonly used in pet therapy, a variety of other animals can be used with positive results. Fish in an aquarium can lower stress, and birds can also be effective. Horses and dolphins are used for pet therapy for autistic children. Female older cats are more difficult to place in homes since everyone wants cute little kittens so that is what I adopt. I am working on taming my 8th cat from the shelter as I write this. The benefits of having animals are numerous for the right owner and we have great indoor and outdoor spaces for a large cat family.

Gardens and Atriums

Another area to explore besides pets to gain life balance is gardens and atriums. Roger Ulrich, Ph.D. has written about the health benefits of gardens in hospitals.

The belief that plants and gardens are beneficial for patients in healthcare environments is more than one thousand years old, and appears prominently in Asian and Western cultures (Ulrich and Parsons, 1992). Stress and psychosocial factors can significantly affect patient health outcomes and should be given high priority along with traditional concerns, including infection risk exposure and functional efficiency, in governing the design of hospitals (Ulrich 2001). Indoor and outdoor gardens and atriums have a calming effect on people. Many big cities have outdoor gardens open to the public. Some of them are specialty gardens such as the International Rose Test Garden in Portland, Oregon and the Oregon Garden in Silverton, Oregon. The Butchart Gardens located on Vancouver Island are over 100 years old and are a great way to spend the day. In addition, 300 acres, a 20-room conservatory, 20 outdoor gardens, and the Heritage Exhibit in the Peirce-duPont House constitute the Longwood Gardens in Kennett Square, Pennsylvania.

Another garden is the Clark Gardens Botanical Park in Weatherford, Texas. There are a lot of atriums and indoor garden plazas to enjoy during the winter. Visiting gardens and observing all of nature's bounties have a calming effect on us.

Wellbeing

In thinking about life balance, the book ***Wellbeing: The Five Essential Elements***, by Rath and Harter (2010) is Gallup's comprehensive study of people in more than 150 countries. It revealed five universal, interconnected elements that shape our lives: career wellbeing, social wellbeing, financial wellbeing, physical wellbeing and community wellbeing. At its simplest level, wellbeing is perhaps ultimately about personal happiness, feeling good, and living safely and healthily. This means not allowing work to undermine our basic purposes and needs in our lives and by extension those of our families and loved ones. The surveys were classified into three areas: thriving, struggling, and suffering. Daily decisions affect our long-term wellbeing and make the difference in our ability to thrive, rather than struggle or suffer. Wellbeing and personal and career values are inextricably intertwined.

Career Wellbeing

In the book, career wellbeing is defined as doing what you love to do and has the largest effect on our lives due to the time spent working. For those engaged in workplace activities, happiness and interest throughout the day were higher than those with low engagement, whose happiness increased towards the end of the day. Career wellbeing is highest when people love their work so much it positively affects their personal lives. There is evidence that boosting career wellbeing might also reduce the risk of anxiety and depression as well as improve physical health. Recommendations include: use your strengths every day, spend more time with someone who has a shared mission, and opt into more social time with the people and teams you enjoy being around. Those with high career wellbeing are twice as likely to be thriving in their lives overall.

Social Wellbeing

Social wellbeing influences our habits, behaviors, and health and is dependent upon our entire network. Indirect connections, including your friend's friend, influence your social wellbeing. Three recommendations for boosting social wellbeing include spending six hours a day (including time at work, at home, on the phone, or engaged in email and other communication) socializing with friends, family and colleagues. Strengthen the mutual connections in your network. Mix social time with physical activity such as a long walk.

Physical Wellbeing

Physical wellbeing is about health, longevity, feeling better, looking better and the energy to get things done on a daily basis. Three recommendations for enhancing physical wellbeing include daily physical activity to improve your mood throughout the day, enough sleep to feel well-rested (seven to eight hours, but not more than nine hours), and grocery shopping habits that include loading up on natural foods that are dark red, green, or blue.

Financial Wellbeing

Financial wellbeing is effective management of your economic life. Financial security has more influence on your overall wellbeing than your income alone. Research has found that at almost every income level, experiential purchases produce a higher level of wellbeing than material purchases because material items fade, but experiences can be relived forever. As income levels increase, experiential purchases produce two to three times the levels of wellbeing when compared to material purchases. Three recommendations for boosting financial wellbeing include buying experiences -- such as vacations and outings with friends or loved ones, spending on others instead of solely on material possessions, and establishing default systems such as automated payments and savings that lessen daily worry about money.

In the eighth lesson, furry friends, gardens and different types of wellbeing was discussed. How we feel ties back to the first lesson on emotions and how we function especially financially.

LESSON 9 CHOICES

In the ninth lesson, the choices were make are considered from an immediate perspective and life or long-term perspective

There are challenges at every decade in your life. In your 20s, it's all about you, the individual, until a relationship comes along. In your 30s, it may be about having a family and purchasing a house. Raising teens and getting them launched in your 40s is a significant challenge; in your 50s, you may face an empty nest. In your 60s, you may be phasing into retirement and creating a different lifestyle with friends. Each decade requires adjustments – both financially and emotionally to deal with the new challenges. Some people have positive personalities and try to make the best use of their time by contributing to society. While hard work is an essential component of building wealth, it's possible to work hard for years and have not much to show for it in terms of net worth due to poor decisions and frivolous spending. Others spend their time talking about things they are going to do but avoid making important decisions. The possibilities are endless, but it all comes down to decisions and choices of time and money in their lives.

Perspective

In an article, *Your Perception is Your Reality*, the way you are viewed and present yourself is the impression you will leave behind. You are in charge of your appearance, personality and capabilities, or how you are perceived by others. What people perceive and believe is based upon hearing, seeing and thinking of others. The self-fulfilling prophecy refers to a statement that alters actions and therefore becomes true. *"Change the ways you look at things and the things you look at change,*" is the essence of the article. A similar article,

Perception is everything in life, "It's not what you physically look at that matter in life, and it's what you see in it." You perceive and respond to life differently through different lenses of experience and values. What one person thinks is an opportunity may be considered a stressor by another, while still others may feel they have life balance. Deciding what is good for you in your life takes time because it involves your feelings and emotions. Gratitude for what we have in life helps with feeling like we have a good life balance.

Six Hats Perspective Tool

1) White Hat: With this thinking hat on, you focus on the data available. Look at the information you have, and see what you can learn from it. Look for gaps in your knowledge, and either try to fill them or take account of them. This is where you analyze past trends and try to extrapolate from historical data.

2) Red Hat: Wearing the red hat, you look at problems using intuition, gut reactions, and emotion. Also try to think how other people will react emotionally. Try to understand the responses of people who do not fully know your reasoning.

3) Yellow Hat: The yellow hat helps you to think positively. It is the optimistic viewpoint that helps you to see all the benefits of the decision and the value in it. Yellow hat thinking helps you keep going when everything looks gloomy and difficult. My business cards are yellow and so is the inside of my house.

4) Green Hat: The green hat stands for creativity. This is where you can develop creative solutions to a problem. It is a freewheeling way of thinking, in which there is little criticism of ideas. A whole range of creativity tools can help you here.

5) Blue Hat: The blue hat stands for process control. This is the hat worn by people chairing meetings. When running into difficulties because ideas are running dry, they may direct activity into green hat thinking. When contingency plans are needed, they will ask for black hat thinking, etc.

6) Black Hat: Using black hat thinking, you will look at all the bad points of the decision. Look at it cautiously and defensively to see why it might not work. Black hat thinking helps to make your plans tougher and more resilient.

EXAMPLE: Your spouse would like to move to a nicer neighborhood and has found a larger home with a pool that you have always wanted.

White Hat: Examine the data. The house would cost you $1,000 more per month, for 30 years, including property taxes. There's also pool maintenance and additional water. Interest rates are at a historical low and will probably rise in the next few years. Neither of you has gotten a raise in the past six years working for the state. The additional debt would increase the debt load to 36%.

Red Hat: Use your intuition. The household budget is tight, especially on high heating and cooling months and your property taxes will be higher next year.

Blue Hat: Engage in process control. Houses are selling quickly and this one won't last long.

Yellow Hat: Look on the bright side. The house is a one-of-a-kind find and would make you very happy to live in it. It would definitely be a step up from your current home.

Green Hat: Be creative. If you borrow money from your aunt, empty your savings account, and hock your wedding ring, you will have enough for the additional down payment.

Black Hat: Review all the data. A bigger home in a nicer neighborhood would be great, but it would be a stretch with the monthly additional payment, maxing out the debt, plus repayment of the down payment. The appliances (e.g., oven, dishwasher, refrigerator, etc.) are getting towards the end of their lifespan. One of your vehicles is getting pretty old too and may need replacing. You and your spouse decide to try to save $1,000 a month for the next few years and see how it goes.

Six hats is tool to give you a rounded or full perspective when making a decision. Gather as much information as possible and enlist help from your colleagues and friends when making large decisions.

Opportunity Costs

What is the cost of the decision? Attending college-really?

An opportunity cost is defined as the value of a forgone activity or alternative when another item or activity is chosen. Opportunity cost comes into play in any decision that involves a tradeoff between two or more options. It is expressed as the relative cost of one alternative in terms of the next best alternative. Opportunity costs are often overlooked in personal decision making. For example, to define the costs of a college education, a student would probably include such costs as tuition, housing, and books. These expenses are examples of accounting or monetary costs of college, but they by no means provide an all-inclusive list of costs. There are many opportunity costs that have been ignored: Wages that could have been earned during the time spent attending class, the value of four years of job experience given up to go to school, the value of any activities missed in order to allocate time to studying, and the value of items that could have been purchased with tuition money or the interest the money could have earned over four years. Opportunity costs are higher for individuals who had good paying jobs and returned to college since that includes no contributions to pension plans and Social Security.

Another example of opportunity costs is the choice to be a stay-at-home mom or dad. Their work at home is worth at least minimum wage plus contributions to Social Security. These opportunity costs may have significant value even though they may not have a specific monetary value. The decision maker must often subjectively estimate opportunity costs. Even though they do not appear on a balance sheet or income statement as expenses, opportunity costs are real because time is a limited resource and needs to be accounted for. Because opportunity costs frequently relate to future events, they are often difficult to quantify. Most decisions have an opportunity cost that is usually not factored in.

Cost Versus Benefit Analysis

Another tool to make a decision is cost/benefit analyses. Costs are quantifiable, while benefits may be either calculated or intangible (i.e., no physical substance), which may include emotions.

The rule is that benefits should exceed the costs.

However, people purchase items with emotions because they want them. For examples, a pet, a different degree, or a house closer to work might be emotional purchases. The cost or amount involved is one constraint. Time is another constraint, since no one has forever to make a choice. It depends on the situation, but don't spend forever in the grocery store – you're spending time versus money. Take your time and ask a lot of questions before making a purchase. Do lots of research to get the best deal for your money, and don't feel intimidated. Make sure you feel right about the decision.

In the ninth and final lesson, choices are examined with different tools starting with one's own perspective and Six Hats. Opportunity costs, Benefits versus cost analysis were added as additional tools for decision making to make better life choices. Hindsight is always 20/20 but we don't make decisions with all the information. Rather, using the information and resources we have at the time to make the best decisions throughout your live time.

May you always prosper with a lifetime of happiness☺

www.ingramcontent.com/pod-product-compliance
Lightning Source LLC
Chambersburg PA
CBHW030815180526
45163CB00003B/1292